PEOPLE IN ANTARCTICA

ANTARCTICA

Lynn M. Stone

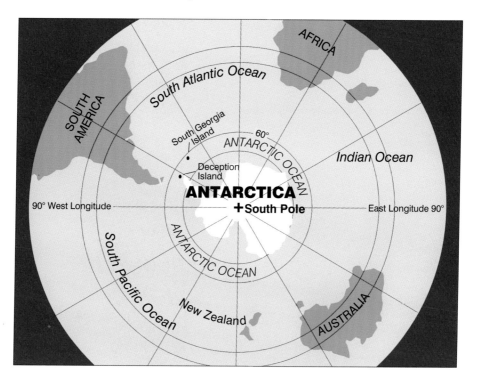

The Rourke Book Co., Inc.
Vero Beach, Florida 32964

PHOTO CREDITS
All photos © Lynn M. Stone except pages 8 (Paul Carrara), 12 and
13 (W.B. Hamilton) courtesy of U.S. Geological Survey

Library of Congress Cataloging-in-Publication Data

Stone, Lynn M.
    People of Antarctica / by Lynn M. Stone.
        p. cm. — (Antarctica)
    Includes index.
    ISBN 1-55916-142-6
    1. Antarctica—Discovery and exploration—Juvenile literature.
2. Explorers—Juvenile literature.   I. Title II. Series: Stone, Lynn M.
Antarctica.
G863.S77 1995
919.8' 9—dc20   95–6894
                                                              CIP
                                                              AC

Printed in the USA

TABLE OF CONTENTS

PEOPLE IN ANTARCTICA

Antarctica is unlike the other six continents in many ways. For one thing, Antarctica has never had its own human population. People do visit Antarctica, but no one has ever lived there for long.

Nearly all of Antarctica is covered by thick ice and mountains. The wind howls, and the temperature drops to more than 100 degrees (Fahrenheit) below zero!

Antarctica is surrounded by a ring of ice. Long ago, people could not even reach Antarctica.

Antarctic shores of snow and ice dwarf a boat carrying tourists

EARLY EXPLORERS

The first person to see Antarctica was probably Thaddeus von Belingshausen, a Russian sailor. Von Belingshausen's ship passed near the frozen, white continent in January, 1820.

For many years explorers could not be sure there was a "new" continent. The wide ring of sea ice around Antarctica kept their wooden ships away. Finally, in 1895, the crew of a whale hunting ship made the first landing on the mainland of Antarctica.

A ring of ice kept early explorers and their wooden ships away from the mainland of Antarctica

LATER EXPLORERS

Many explorers sailed to Antarctica in the early 1900's. They faced many hardships from the cold, wind and ice. Ernest Shackleton's wooden ship was crushed by ice that surrounded it. Shackleton and his men, however, survived.

In 1912 Roald Amundsen led a small group of men across Antarctica to the Earth's **South Pole** (SOUTH POLE). Amundsen's group returned safely. A month later, Robert Scott's team reached the South Pole. They froze to death on their return.

The United States doesn't own the South Pole, but it has a research station there

SEALERS

James Cook, the great English explorer, never saw the mainland of Antarctica. He journeyed in Antarctic seas, however, in the 1770's.

Cook returned to England with stories of huge numbers of seals. Seal hunters soon sailed south to Antarctic islands where the seals came ashore.

For nearly 100 years they killed Antarctic seals for their fur and **blubber** (BLUH ber), or fat. They boiled the seal blubber—and later the blubber of penguins—for its oil.

Nineteenth century seal hunters almost wiped out southern fur seals from the Antarctic region

After World War II, aircraft helped the United States and other nations explore
and map Antarctica

A scientist uses a rope to explore a crack in an Antarctic ice field

WHALERS

Whale ships followed the sealers to the Antarctic. Whales were especially prized for their blubber oil. Animal oils were used as fuel and grease throughout the 1800's and into the 1900's.

In the early 1900's steam-driven boats and a deadly new type of **harpoon** (har POON) made whale hunting much easier than it had been. By the 1950's many kinds of whales were nearly **extinct** (ex TINKT)—gone forever.

The Antarctic whaling business was finished.

Its harpoon forever at rest, the whale ship Petrel lies rusting away at Grytviken, a former whaling port on South Georgia Island

SCIENTISTS

After World War II (1939-1945), airplanes helped scientists map and explore much of Antarctica. Today many nations have **research** (REE serch) stations in the Antarctic.

About 4,000 people, most of them scientists, live at Antarctic stations during the summer. Perhaps no more than 800 spend the Antarctic winter there.

Scientists want to learn more about Antarctica's past, present and future.

An Argentine research station is tucked onto the shore of the Antarctic peninsula

RESEARCH

Scientists look closely at Antarctica's ocean, animals, ice, air, plants, rocks and soil. They use airplanes, snowmobiles, computers and satellites to help with their studies, or research. Scientists sometimes work from small boats, walk great distances and climb with ropes and ice axes.

One discovery of Antarctic scientists is that Antarctica long ago was moist and warm!

A topic of major interest now is the hole in the layer of **ozone** (O zone) high above Antarctica.

British scientists studying Antarctic penguins huddle with their subjects during a snowstorm

GLOBAL WARMING

Scientists also want to know more about "global warming." Many scientists believe that the Earth (globe) is slowly warming. They believe that fuel exhausts, or wastes, are causing a change in the makeup of our air. The "new" air traps more heat from the sun, causing warming temperatures worldwide.

Antarctica has nine-tenths of the world's ice. If it begins to melt, it will raise ocean levels everywhere.

A meltdown of Antarctic ice would raise ocean levels worldwide

PROTECTING ANTARCTICA

Antarctica is a special place. No one owns it, but several countries are interested in its welfare.

These countries have signed the Antarctic Treaty, which lasts until 2042. The Treaty protects Antarctica's plants and animals. It sets aside several areas for the use of scientists only.

The Treaty also prevents anyone from trying to "own" a part of Antarctica or from putting weapons there.

Glossary

blubber (BLUH ber) — a layer of fat which helps keep animals warm in cold climates

extinct (ex TINKT) — no longer existing

harpoon (har POON) — a spearlike object fired or hurled from ships into whales

ozone (O zone) — a form of oxygen found naturally in the upper level of air and useful in helping to block harmful sun rays

research (REE serch) — careful study of something or the information that results from that study

South Pole (SOUTH POLE) — the southernmost point of the Earth, located on Antarctica

INDEX